This Journal Belongs To

THE POWER OF POSITIVITY

Dr. Mary Welsh
www.drmarywelsh.com
www.susieqskids.org

Journey into the Looking Glass:

The Four Aspects of Positive Reflection Journal

You Got This!

Remember ✿ Reflect Recreate ✿ Relate

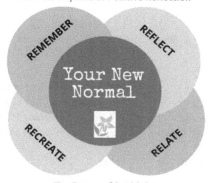

The Four Aspects of Positive Reflection

Your New Normal

The Power of Positivity

Journey into the Looking Glass:
The Four Aspects of Positive Reflection Journal

Author Dr. Mary Welsh

Journey into the Looking Glass:
The Four Aspects of Positive Reflection Journal © 2020
by Dr. Mary Welsh. All rights reserved.

Printed in the United States of America
Published by Author Academy Elite
PO Box 43, Powell, OH 43035
www.AuthorAcademyElite.com

Identifiers:
ISBN: 978-1-64746-230-7 (paperback)

Available in paperback.

Journey into the Looking Glass:
Four Aspects of Positive Reflection Journal

Author Dr. Mary Welsh

Additional Works by Dr Mary Welsh

*Journey into the Looking Glass: Finding Hope after
the Loss of Loved Ones* (adult grieving book)
Susie Q's Kids Positive Reflections: My Special Angel
(children's grief book)
Susie Q's Kids Positive Reflections: Good Characteristics
(children's coloring book)

Dr. Mary Welsh
www.drmarywelsh.com
www.susieqskids.org

DR. MARY WELSH

EMBRACE THE POWER OF POSITIVITY

D r. Welsh co-founded the non-profit Susie Q's Kids following the death of her daughter, Susie McBride-Welsh. Susie Q's Kids raises awareness for other non-profits which distributes their comfort bags to hospitals, foster care, shelters, and those grieving "One Bag at a Time" brightening and inspiring the lives of children and young adults.

She took her tragedy, passion, and purpose, and created a stage for positive interactions with children, young adults, family, friends, and those grieving the loss of a loved one or facing adverse situations through her positive perspective, purpose, teachings, and interactions. Her hope is they find peace with their "new normal."

As a Grief Sessions Facilitator, Author, Coach, National Speaker she documented the first two years of her journey for people who have suffered the loss of a child or loved one or supporting those that are experiencing such a loss. Her goal is to support their grief journey with information and provide a program to guide them on their journey. Her speaking engagements include:

- ♦ Compassionate Friends National Speaker
- ♦ Bereaved Parents of USA National Speaker

Her literary works include:

- ♦ *Journey into the Looking Glass: Finding Hope after the Loss of Loved One* (adult grief book)
- ♦ *Susie Q's Kids Positive Reflections: My Special Angel* (children's grief book)

♦ *Susie Q's Kids Positive Reflections: Good Characteristics* (children's coloring book)

She also acts as a Tragedy Assistance Program for Survivors (TAPS) Peer Mentor for fallen military survivors providing guidance, support, and companionship to those in the grieving process.

As a Grief Session Facilitator, Author, National Speaker, Entrepreneur, University Professor, Business Strategist, HR Talent Executive, and Chief People Person, she has a passion and purpose for helping others. Through her writing, mentoring, courses, and speaking engagements, she hopes to instill a framework for grievers and those facing adversity to find comfort in their new circumstances and a life of passion and purpose.

Dr. Mary is happily married to her husband, Joseph Welsh, with six amazing children and five awesome grandchildren that fill her life with happiness as well as being surrounded by her cherished mother, mother-in-law, father-in-law, and a tribe of loving family and friends.

HOW TO REMAIN POSITIVE IN THE FACE OF ADVERSITY

THE FOUR ASPECTS OF POSITIVE REFLECTION

The Four Aspects of Positive Reflection embraces the power of positivity and allows individuals to find the right path to face the adversities of life and embrace their "new normal" whether it is due to the loss of a loved one, divorce, personal challenge, health issue, or other adversity.

Although the ache of losing a loved one cannot be escaped, it can be a catalyst for positive change. In her book, *Journey into the Looking Glass: Finding Hope after the Loss of Loved Ones*, Dr. Mary described the loss of her daughter Susie, her relationship, the grief process, and how she harnessed the worst moments in her life to create a transparent book of her journey and self-help and discovery topics to aid others in their grieving process. Her strength comes from sharing her story and the hope that others find solace and inspiration on their own journeys with the passion for leading purposeful lives

- **Remember**: Understand Your Past and How Your Loved Ones Impacted You - Remember the Good and Bad Memories
- **Reflect**: Understand Your Journey and Path to Grasping the Impact You Had on Your Loved Ones and They Had on You
- **Recreate**: Get in Touch with Your Feelings and Come to Grips with Them - Embrace Your New Normal
- **Relate**: Make Your Commitment to Living and Your "New Normal" - Practice Self-care, Supporting Others, and Giving Back in the Community

Remember: Understand Your Past - Your life has changed forever, and memories will always fill it with a sense of loss for what is missing from your life. It will be your "New Normal."

To understand my approach, I shared some stories about my daughter, Susan McBride-Welsh (Susie Q), and a tribute from her dad, Joseph Welsh. I encourage you to do the same. It provides an anchor for where we came from, the good times, and the well of hope that can feed our injured souls. Although the journey will have ups and downs, by designing a clear picture of our past, it will lead us to a closer destination of hope, inspiration, passion, and purpose. The first step toward getting there is asking for help. In this journal, define your journey and a potential roadmap of self-discovery to consider your next move.

Reflect: Understand Your Journey - Nothing ever goes exactly according to plan; your journey will take you through the stages of grief in no particular order. The gut-wrenching sorrow can hit you at any time. Understanding the stages are normal may provide you with some techniques to get you through your moments. It is about understanding things are different. We must learn to move forward never forgetting their life and contributions but learning how to live a life without their physical presence. The most crucial aspect is self-care, working through *Journey into the Looking Glass: Finding Hope after the Loss of Loved Ones* book is a step in the right direction. Be open, be honest with others, don't be afraid to speak up, to take care of your needs, to say "no," to whatever. It is your journey and thus personal to you and your feelings, practice self-care to get in tune with your feelings.

MAKE YOUR 'NEW NORMAL' THE BEST

YOU GOT THIS!

Recreate: Get in Touch with Your Feelings – "What If is a dangerous statement. These "What If" statements can play with our emotions daily as we reminisce about days gone by etched in our memories. We long for the current day vacancies, voids, and hopes as well as the future wishes that will never come true. Learning to cope with them and remembering their loss and your own losses can be daunting as you create your "New Normal." Practice identifying your "What If" statement and replace them with "But I/we Did" statements. This technique challenged my thought patterns to reflect on the positive side of "What If" statements and the actions and relationships that impact my approach to life.

Relate: Make Your Commitment to Your "New Normal"– Loss happens in many different ways and impacts each of us differently. Look at your situation, what you can do, what you can commit to doing, the people in your life to aid you, and the people in your life you need to support. Learn that everyone grieves differently. Devote your actions to make a commitment and impact on growing and healing. Expressing your grief with others makes it more palatable, it allows you to connect and find solace in their relationship with you and enables you to establish guidelines to make life more acceptable and purposeful.

Dr. Mary Welsh

Author, Speaker, Grief Session Facilitator,
Non-Profit Co-Founder, University Professor

5

Q's THUMBS-UP REVOLUTION

Q's Thumbs Up Revolution - Be Inspired

Imagine a life full of positivity and an appreciation for the past, the present, and the future. A simple gesture such as a "thumbs-up" can signify 'you can do it' or 'good job', and provide positive reinforcement.

Our family and friends extend a thumbs-up in our photo opportunities to recognize our loved one. Susie is with us always. When we look back on the pictures, we can see her in all our life's events captured in our pictures with a simple thumbs-up gesture.

Join the Thumbs Up Revolution. Post your pictures and a brief caption of the event or person recognized with your thumbs up.

Learn more visit our website:
www.https://drmarywelsh.com
https://www.facebook.com/Thumbs-Up-Revolution-1073516522838068

Susie "Q" McBride-Welsh

SUSIE Q'S KIDS

"ONE BAG AT A TIME"

Susie Q's Kids was started to honor Susan McBride-Welsh (Susie Q) a special young lady who loved kids, giving back, and living every day to its fullest. All kids suffering health issues, inconsistent living arrangements, and grieving need comfort. Imagine the smile as the kids we help find inspiration and comfort in the contents of our special comfort bags. They matter.

Susie Q's Kids is committed to brightening and inspiring the lives of children and young adults, "One Bag at a Time." Make a difference, support our cause, every contribution helps to brighten and inspire the lives of a child or young adult. Our bags are provided to other nonprofits for distribution to their program participants in hospitals, foster care, shelters, and those grieving.

Learn more by visiting our website:
https://susieqskids.org/
https://drmarywelsh.com/

REMEMBER ✿ REFLECT ✿ RECREATE ✿ RELATE

SHARE YOUR THOUGHTS TODAY

How did you remember, reflect, recreate, and relate today?

_____

_____

_____

_____

_____

_____

_____

_____

What did you do for yourself today?

_____

_____

_____

_____

_____

_____

What did you do for others today?

_____

_____

_____

_____

_____

_____

REMEMBER ❀ REFLECT ❀ RECREATE ❀ RELATE
SHARE YOUR THOUGHTS TODAY

How did you remember, reflect, recreate, and relate today?

_____

_____

_____

_____

_____

_____

_____

What did you do for yourself today?

_____

_____

_____

_____

_____

What did you do for others today?

_____

_____

_____

_____

_____

_____

REMEMBER ❁ REFLECT ❁ RECREATE ❁ RELATE
SHARE YOUR THOUGHTS TODAY

How did you remember, reflect, recreate, and relate today?

What did you do for yourself today?

What did you do for others today?

REMEMBER ❁ REFLECT ❁ RECREATE ❁ RELATE

How did you remember, reflect, recreate, and relate today?

_____

_____

_____

_____

_____

_____

_____

_____

What did you do for yourself today?

_____

_____

_____

_____

_____

_____

_____

What did you do for others today?

_____

_____

_____

_____

_____

_____

_____

REMEMBER ✸ REFLECT ✸ RECREATE ✸ RELATE

SHARE YOUR THOUGHTS TODAY

How did you remember, reflect, recreate, and relate today?

What did you do for yourself today?

What did you do for others today?

REMEMBER ✿ REFLECT ✿ RECREATE ✿ RELATE

SHARE YOUR THOUGHTS TODAY

How did you remember, reflect, recreate, and relate today?

What did you do for yourself today?

What did you do for others today?

REMEMBER ❊ REFLECT ❊ RECREATE ❊ RELATE

SHARE YOUR THOUGHTS TODAY

How did you remember, reflect, recreate, and relate today?

What did you do for yourself today?

What did you do for others today?

REMEMBER ✿ REFLECT ✿ RECREATE ✿ RELATE

How did you remember, reflect, recreate, and relate today?

_____

_____

_____

_____

_____

_____

_____

What did you do for yourself today?

_____

_____

_____

_____

_____

_____

What did you do for others today?

_____

_____

_____

_____

_____

_____

_____

REMEMBER ❀ REFLECT ❀ RECREATE ❀ RELATE

SHARE YOUR THOUGHTS TODAY

How did you remember, reflect, recreate, and relate today?

What did you do for yourself today?

What did you do for others today?

REMEMBER ❀ REFLECT ❀ RECREATE ❀ RELATE

SHARE YOUR THOUGHTS TODAY

How did you remember, reflect, recreate, and relate today?

What did you do for yourself today?

What did you do for others today?

REMEMBER ❀ REFLECT ❀ RECREATE ❀ RELATE

SHARE YOUR THOUGHTS TODAY

How did you remember, reflect, recreate, and relate today?

What did you do for yourself today?

What did you do for others today?

REMEMBER ❀ REFLECT ❀ RECREATE ❀ RELATE

SHARE YOUR THOUGHTS TODAY

How did you remember, reflect, recreate, and relate today?

What did you do for yourself today?

What did you do for others today?

REMEMBER ❀ REFLECT ❀ RECREATE ❀ RELATE

SHARE YOUR THOUGHTS TODAY

How did you remember, reflect, recreate, and relate today?

_____
_____
_____
_____
_____
_____
_____

What did you do for yourself today?

_____
_____
_____
_____
_____
_____
_____

What did you do for others today?

_____
_____
_____
_____
_____
_____
_____

REMEMBER ❀ REFLECT ❀ RECREATE ❀ RELATE

How did you remember, reflect, recreate, and relate today?

What did you do for yourself today?

What did you do for others today?

REMEMBER ❀ REFLECT ❀ RECREATE ❀ RELATE

SHARE YOUR THOUGHTS TODAY

How did you remember, reflect, recreate, and relate today?

What did you do for yourself today?

What did you do for others today?

REMEMBER ❋ REFLECT ❋ RECREATE ❋ RELATE

How did you remember, reflect, recreate, and relate today?

What did you do for yourself today?

What did you do for others today?

REMEMBER ❄ REFLECT ❄ RECREATE ❄ RELATE

How did you remember, reflect, recreate, and relate today?

What did you do for yourself today?

What did you do for others today?

REMEMBER ❀ REFLECT ❀ RECREATE ❀ RELATE
SHARE YOUR THOUGHTS TODAY

How did you remember, reflect, recreate, and relate today?

What did you do for yourself today?

What did you do for others today?

REMEMBER ❀ REFLECT ❀ RECREATE ❀ RELATE

SHARE YOUR THOUGHTS TODAY

How did you remember, reflect, recreate, and relate today?

What did you do for yourself today?

What did you do for others today?

REMEMBER ❀ REFLECT ❀ RECREATE ❀ RELATE

SHARE YOUR THOUGHTS TODAY

How did you remember, reflect, recreate, and relate today?

What did you do for yourself today?

What did you do for others today?

REMEMBER ❀ REFLECT ❀ RECREATE ❀ RELATE

SHARE YOUR THOUGHTS TODAY

How did you remember, reflect, recreate, and relate today?

What did you do for yourself today?

What did you do for others today?

REMEMBER ❀ REFLECT ❀ RECREATE ❀ RELATE

SHARE YOUR THOUGHTS TODAY

How did you remember, reflect, recreate, and relate today?

_____

_____

_____

_____

_____

_____

_____

_____

_____

What did you do for yourself today?

_____

_____

_____

_____

_____

_____

_____

What did you do for others today?

_____

_____

_____

_____

_____

_____

_____

REMEMBER ❀ REFLECT ❀ RECREATE ❀ RELATE

SHARE YOUR THOUGHTS TODAY

How did you remember, reflect, recreate, and relate today?

What did you do for yourself today?

What did you do for others today?

REMEMBER ❁ REFLECT ❁ RECREATE ❁ RELATE

SHARE YOUR THOUGHTS TODAY

How did you remember, reflect, recreate, and relate today?

What did you do for yourself today?

What did you do for others today?

REMEMBER ✿ REFLECT ✿ RECREATE ✿ RELATE

SHARE YOUR THOUGHTS TODAY

How did you remember, reflect, recreate, and relate today?

What did you do for yourself today?

What did you do for others today?

REMEMBER ❀ REFLECT ❀ RECREATE ❀ RELATE

SHARE YOUR THOUGHTS TODAY

How did you remember, reflect, recreate, and relate today?

What did you do for yourself today?

What did you do for others today?

REMEMBER ✿ REFLECT ✿ RECREATE ✿ RELATE

SHARE YOUR THOUGHTS TODAY

How did you remember, reflect, recreate, and relate today?

_____

_____

_____

_____

_____

_____

_____

_____

What did you do for yourself today?

_____

_____

_____

_____

_____

_____

_____

What did you do for others today?

_____

_____

_____

_____

_____

_____

_____

REMEMBER ❄ REFLECT ❄ RECREATE ❄ RELATE

SHARE YOUR THOUGHTS TODAY

How did you remember, reflect, recreate, and relate today?

What did you do for yourself today?

What did you do for others today?

REMEMBER ❀ REFLECT ❀ RECREATE ❀ RELATE

How did you remember, reflect, recreate, and relate today?

What did you do for yourself today?

What did you do for others today?

REMEMBER ✿ REFLECT ✿ RECREATE ✿ RELATE

SHARE YOUR THOUGHTS TODAY

How did you remember, reflect, recreate, and relate today?

What did you do for yourself today?

What did you do for others today?

REMEMBER ❀ REFLECT ❀ RECREATE ❀ RELATE

SHARE YOUR THOUGHTS TODAY

How did you remember, reflect, recreate, and relate today?

What did you do for yourself today?

What did you do for others today?

REMEMBER ❀ REFLECT ❀ RECREATE ❀ RELATE

SHARE YOUR THOUGHTS TODAY

How did you remember, reflect, recreate, and relate today?

What did you do for yourself today?

What did you do for others today?

REMEMBER ❃ REFLECT ❃ RECREATE ❃ RELATE

SHARE YOUR THOUGHTS TODAY

How did you remember, reflect, recreate, and relate today?

_____

_____

_____

_____

_____

_____

_____

_____

What did you do for yourself today?

_____

_____

_____

_____

_____

_____

_____

What did you do for others today?

_____

_____

_____

_____

_____

_____

_____

_____

REMEMBER ❀ REFLECT ❀ RECREATE ❀ RELATE

SHARE YOUR THOUGHTS TODAY

How did you remember, reflect, recreate, and relate today?

What did you do for yourself today?

What did you do for others today?

REMEMBER ❀ REFLECT ❀ RECREATE ❀ RELATE

SHARE YOUR THOUGHTS TODAY

How did you remember, reflect, recreate, and relate today?

What did you do for yourself today?

What did you do for others today?

REMEMBER ✿ REFLECT ✿ RECREATE ✿ RELATE

SHARE YOUR THOUGHTS TODAY

How did you remember, reflect, recreate, and relate today?

What did you do for yourself today?

What did you do for others today?

REMEMBER ❄ REFLECT ❄ RECREATE ❄ RELATE

SHARE YOUR THOUGHTS TODAY

How did you remember, reflect, recreate, and relate today?

What did you do for yourself today?

What did you do for others today?

REMEMBER ✿ REFLECT ✿ RECREATE ✿ RELATE

SHARE YOUR THOUGHTS TODAY

How did you remember, reflect, recreate, and relate today?

What did you do for yourself today?

What did you do for others today?

REMEMBER ❀ REFLECT ❀ RECREATE ❀ RELATE

SHARE YOUR THOUGHTS TODAY

How did you remember, reflect, recreate, and relate today?

What did you do for yourself today?

What did you do for others today?

REMEMBER ❀ REFLECT ❀ RECREATE ❀ RELATE

SHARE YOUR THOUGHTS TODAY

How did you remember, reflect, recreate, and relate today?

What did you do for yourself today?

What did you do for others today?

REMEMBER ❀ REFLECT ❀ RECREATE ❀ RELATE

SHARE YOUR THOUGHTS TODAY

How did you remember, reflect, recreate, and relate today?

What did you do for yourself today?

What did you do for others today?

REMEMBER ❀ REFLECT ❀ RECREATE ❀ RELATE

SHARE YOUR THOUGHTS TODAY

How did you remember, reflect, recreate, and relate today?

_____
_____
_____
_____
_____
_____
_____
_____

What did you do for yourself today?

_____
_____
_____
_____
_____
_____
_____

What did you do for others today?

_____
_____
_____
_____
_____
_____
_____

REMEMBER ❀ REFLECT ❀ RECREATE ❀ RELATE

SHARE YOUR THOUGHTS TODAY

How did you remember, reflect, recreate, and relate today?

What did you do for yourself today?

What did you do for others today?

REMEMBER ❀ REFLECT ❀ RECREATE ❀ RELATE
SHARE YOUR THOUGHTS TODAY

How did you remember, reflect, recreate, and relate today?

What did you do for yourself today?

What did you do for others today?

REMEMBER ❀ REFLECT ❀ RECREATE ❀ RELATE

SHARE YOUR THOUGHTS TODAY

How did you remember, reflect, recreate, and relate today?

What did you do for yourself today?

What did you do for others today?

REMEMBER ❀ REFLECT ❀ RECREATE ❀ RELATE

SHARE YOUR THOUGHTS TODAY

How did you remember, reflect, recreate, and relate today?

What did you do for yourself today?

What did you do for others today?

REMEMBER ❀ REFLECT ❀ RECREATE ❀ RELATE

SHARE YOUR THOUGHTS TODAY

How did you remember, reflect, recreate, and relate today?

What did you do for yourself today?

What did you do for others today?

REMEMBER ❀ REFLECT ❀ RECREATE ❀ RELATE

SHARE YOUR THOUGHTS TODAY

How did you remember, reflect, recreate, and relate today?

What did you do for yourself today?

What did you do for others today?

REMEMBER ❀ REFLECT ❀ RECREATE ❀ RELATE

SHARE YOUR THOUGHTS TODAY

How did you remember, reflect, recreate, and relate today?

What did you do for yourself today?

What did you do for others today?

REMEMBER ❀ REFLECT ❀ RECREATE ❀ RELATE

SHARE YOUR THOUGHTS TODAY

How did you remember, reflect, recreate, and relate today?

What did you do for yourself today?

What did you do for others today?

REMEMBER ❀ REFLECT ❀ RECREATE ❀ RELATE

SHARE YOUR THOUGHTS TODAY

How did you remember, reflect, recreate, and relate today?

What did you do for yourself today?

What did you do for others today?

REMEMBER ✿ REFLECT ✿ RECREATE ✿ RELATE

How did you remember, reflect, recreate, and relate today?

What did you do for yourself today?

What did you do for others today?

REMEMBER ❀ REFLECT ❀ RECREATE ❀ RELATE

SHARE YOUR THOUGHTS TODAY

How did you remember, reflect, recreate, and relate today?

_____

_____

_____

_____

_____

_____

_____

_____

What did you do for yourself today?

_____

_____

_____

_____

_____

_____

What did you do for others today?

_____

_____

_____

_____

_____

_____

_____

REMEMBER ❁ REFLECT ❁ RECREATE ❁ RELATE

SHARE YOUR THOUGHTS TODAY

How did you remember, reflect, recreate, and relate today?

What did you do for yourself today?

What did you do for others today?

REMEMBER ❀ REFLECT ❀ RECREATE ❀ RELATE

SHARE YOUR THOUGHTS TODAY

How did you remember, reflect, recreate, and relate today?

What did you do for yourself today?

What did you do for others today?

REMEMBER ❉ REFLECT ❉ RECREATE ❉ RELATE

How did you remember, reflect, recreate, and relate today?

_____

_____

_____

_____

_____

_____

_____

What did you do for yourself today?

_____

_____

_____

_____

_____

_____

What did you do for others today?

_____

_____

_____

_____

_____

_____

REMEMBER ❀ REFLECT ❀ RECREATE ❀ RELATE

SHARE YOUR THOUGHTS TODAY

How did you remember, reflect, recreate, and relate today?

What did you do for yourself today?

What did you do for others today?

REMEMBER ❀ REFLECT ❀ RECREATE ❀ RELATE

SHARE YOUR THOUGHTS TODAY

How did you remember, reflect, recreate, and relate today?

What did you do for yourself today?

What did you do for others today?

REMEMBER ❀ REFLECT ❀ RECREATE ❀ RELATE

SHARE YOUR THOUGHTS TODAY

How did you remember, reflect, recreate, and relate today?

_____

_____

_____

_____

_____

_____

_____

_____

What did you do for yourself today?

_____

_____

_____

_____

_____

_____

What did you do for others today?

_____

_____

_____

_____

_____

_____

REMEMBER ❀ REFLECT ❀ RECREATE ❀ RELATE

How did you remember, reflect, recreate, and relate today?

_____

_____

_____

_____

_____

_____

_____

_____

What did you do for yourself today?

_____

_____

_____

_____

_____

_____

_____

What did you do for others today?

_____

_____

_____

_____

_____

_____

REMEMBER ❀ REFLECT ❀ RECREATE ❀ RELATE

SHARE YOUR THOUGHTS TODAY

How did you remember, reflect, recreate, and relate today?

_____

_____

_____

_____

_____

_____

_____

What did you do for yourself today?

_____

_____

_____

_____

_____

_____

_____

What did you do for others today?

_____

_____

_____

_____

_____

_____

REMEMBER ❀ REFLECT ❀ RECREATE ❀ RELATE

SHARE YOUR THOUGHTS TODAY

How did you remember, reflect, recreate, and relate today?

What did you do for yourself today?

What did you do for others today?

REMEMBER ✿ REFLECT ✿ RECREATE ✿ RELATE

SHARE YOUR THOUGHTS TODAY

How did you remember, reflect, recreate, and relate today?

What did you do for yourself today?

What did you do for others today?

REMEMBER ❀ REFLECT ❀ RECREATE ❀ RELATE

SHARE YOUR THOUGHTS TODAY

How did you remember, reflect, recreate, and relate today?

What did you do for yourself today?

What did you do for others today?

REMEMBER ❀ REFLECT ❀ RECREATE ❀ RELATE

SHARE YOUR THOUGHTS TODAY

How did you remember, reflect, recreate, and relate today?

What did you do for yourself today?

What did you do for others today?

REMEMBER ✿ REFLECT ✿ RECREATE ✿ RELATE
SHARE YOUR THOUGHTS TODAY

How did you remember, reflect, recreate, and relate today?

What did you do for yourself today?

What did you do for others today?

REMEMBER ❀ REFLECT ❀ RECREATE ❀ RELATE
SHARE YOUR THOUGHTS TODAY

How did you remember, reflect, recreate, and relate today?

What did you do for yourself today?

What did you do for others today?

REMEMBER ❀ REFLECT ❀ RECREATE ❀ RELATE

SHARE YOUR THOUGHTS TODAY

How did you remember, reflect, recreate, and relate today?

What did you do for yourself today?

What did you do for others today?

REMEMBER ❀ REFLECT ❀ RECREATE ❀ RELATE

SHARE YOUR THOUGHTS TODAY

How did you remember, reflect, recreate, and relate today?

What did you do for yourself today?

What did you do for others today?

REMEMBER ❋ REFLECT ❋ RECREATE ❋ RELATE

SHARE YOUR THOUGHTS TODAY

How did you remember, reflect, recreate, and relate today?

What did you do for yourself today?

What did you do for others today?

REMEMBER ✿ REFLECT ✿ RECREATE ✿ RELATE

SHARE YOUR THOUGHTS TODAY

How did you remember, reflect, recreate, and relate today?

What did you do for yourself today?

What did you do for others today?

REMEMBER ❀ REFLECT ❀ RECREATE ❀ RELATE

SHARE YOUR THOUGHTS TODAY

How did you remember, reflect, recreate, and relate today?

What did you do for yourself today?

What did you do for others today?

REMEMBER ❀ REFLECT ❀ RECREATE ❀ RELATE

SHARE YOUR THOUGHTS TODAY

How did you remember, reflect, recreate, and relate today?

What did you do for yourself today?

What did you do for others today?

REMEMBER ❀ REFLECT ❀ RECREATE ❀ RELATE
SHARE YOUR THOUGHTS TODAY

How did you remember, reflect, recreate, and relate today?

What did you do for yourself today?

What did you do for others today?

REMEMBER ✿ REFLECT ✿ RECREATE ✿ RELATE
SHARE YOUR THOUGHTS TODAY

How did you remember, reflect, recreate, and relate today?

What did you do for yourself today?

What did you do for others today?

REMEMBER ❀ REFLECT ❀ RECREATE ❀ RELATE
SHARE YOUR THOUGHTS TODAY

How did you remember, reflect, recreate, and relate today?

What did you do for yourself today?

What did you do for others today?

REMEMBER ✿ REFLECT ✿ RECREATE ✿ RELATE
SHARE YOUR THOUGHTS TODAY

How did you remember, reflect, recreate, and relate today?

What did you do for yourself today?

What did you do for others today?

REMEMBER ❀ REFLECT ❀ RECREATE ❀ RELATE

SHARE YOUR THOUGHTS TODAY

How did you remember, reflect, recreate, and relate today?

What did you do for yourself today?

What did you do for others today?

REMEMBER ❀ REFLECT ❀ RECREATE ❀ RELATE

SHARE YOUR THOUGHTS TODAY

How did you remember, reflect, recreate, and relate today?

What did you do for yourself today?

What did you do for others today?

REMEMBER ✿ REFLECT ✿ RECREATE ✿ RELATE

SHARE YOUR THOUGHTS TODAY

How did you remember, reflect, recreate, and relate today?

What did you do for yourself today?

What did you do for others today?

REMEMBER ❀ REFLECT ❀ RECREATE ❀ RELATE

SHARE YOUR THOUGHTS TODAY

How did you remember, reflect, recreate, and relate today?

What did you do for yourself today?

What did you do for others today?

REMEMBER ❀ REFLECT ❀ RECREATE ❀ RELATE

SHARE YOUR THOUGHTS TODAY

How did you remember, reflect, recreate, and relate today?

What did you do for yourself today?

What did you do for others today?

REMEMBER ❁ REFLECT ❁ RECREATE ❁ RELATE

SHARE YOUR THOUGHTS TODAY

How did you remember, reflect, recreate, and relate today?

What did you do for yourself today?

What did you do for others today?

REMEMBER ❀ REFLECT ❀ RECREATE ❀ RELATE

SHARE YOUR THOUGHTS TODAY

How did you remember, reflect, recreate, and relate today?

What did you do for yourself today?

What did you do for others today?

REMEMBER ❀ REFLECT ❀ RECREATE ❀ RELATE

SHARE YOUR THOUGHTS TODAY

How did you remember, reflect, recreate, and relate today?

What did you do for yourself today?

What did you do for others today?

REMEMBER ❀ REFLECT ❀ RECREATE ❀ RELATE

How did you remember, reflect, recreate, and relate today?

What did you do for yourself today?

What did you do for others today?

REMEMBER ❀ REFLECT ❀ RECREATE ❀ RELATE

How did you remember, reflect, recreate, and relate today?

What did you do for yourself today?

What did you do for others today?

REMEMBER ❀ REFLECT ❀ RECREATE ❀ RELATE

SHARE YOUR THOUGHTS TODAY

How did you remember, reflect, recreate, and relate today?

What did you do for yourself today?

What did you do for others today?

REMEMBER ❋ REFLECT ❋ RECREATE ❋ RELATE

SHARE YOUR THOUGHTS TODAY

How did you remember, reflect, recreate, and relate today?

What did you do for yourself today?

What did you do for others today?

REMEMBER ❀ REFLECT ❀ RECREATE ❀ RELATE

SHARE YOUR THOUGHTS TODAY

How did you remember, reflect, recreate, and relate today?

What did you do for yourself today?

What did you do for others today?

REMEMBER ❀ REFLECT ❀ RECREATE ❀ RELATE

SHARE YOUR THOUGHTS TODAY

How did you remember, reflect, recreate, and relate today?

What did you do for yourself today?

What did you do for others today?

REMEMBER ❀ REFLECT ❀ RECREATE ❀ RELATE

SHARE YOUR THOUGHTS TODAY

How did you remember, reflect, recreate, and relate today?

What did you do for yourself today?

What did you do for others today?

REMEMBER ✿ REFLECT ✿ RECREATE ✿ RELATE

SHARE YOUR THOUGHTS TODAY

How did you remember, reflect, recreate, and relate today?

What did you do for yourself today?

What did you do for others today?

REMEMBER ❉ REFLECT ❉ RECREATE ❉ RELATE
SHARE YOUR THOUGHTS TODAY

How did you remember, reflect, recreate, and relate today?

_____

_____

_____

_____

_____

_____

_____

What did you do for yourself today?

_____

_____

_____

_____

_____

_____

What did you do for others today?

_____

_____

_____

_____

_____

_____

_____

REMEMBER ✿ REFLECT ✿ RECREATE ✿ RELATE

SHARE YOUR THOUGHTS TODAY

How did you remember, reflect, recreate, and relate today?

What did you do for yourself today?

What did you do for others today?

REMEMBER ❀ REFLECT ❀ RECREATE ❀ RELATE

SHARE YOUR THOUGHTS TODAY

How did you remember, reflect, recreate, and relate today?

What did you do for yourself today?

What did you do for others today?

REMEMBER ✿ REFLECT ✿ RECREATE ✿ RELATE

SHARE YOUR THOUGHTS TODAY

How did you remember, reflect, recreate, and relate today?

_____

_____

_____

_____

_____

_____

_____

_____

What did you do for yourself today?

_____

_____

_____

_____

_____

_____

What did you do for others today?

_____

_____

_____

_____

_____

_____

REMEMBER ❀ REFLECT ❀ RECREATE ❀ RELATE

SHARE YOUR THOUGHTS TODAY

How did you remember, reflect, recreate, and relate today?

What did you do for yourself today?

What did you do for others today?

REMEMBER ✾ REFLECT ✾ RECREATE ✾ RELATE

SHARE YOUR THOUGHTS TODAY

How did you remember, reflect, recreate, and relate today?

What did you do for yourself today?

What did you do for others today?

REMEMBER ❀ REFLECT ❀ RECREATE ❀ RELATE

SHARE YOUR THOUGHTS TODAY

How did you remember, reflect, recreate, and relate today?

What did you do for yourself today?

What did you do for others today?

REMEMBER ❀ REFLECT ❀ RECREATE ❀ RELATE

SHARE YOUR THOUGHTS TODAY

How did you remember, reflect, recreate, and relate today?

What did you do for yourself today?

What did you do for others today?

REMEMBER ❋ REFLECT ❋ RECREATE ❋ RELATE

How did you remember, reflect, recreate, and relate today?

_____
_____
_____
_____
_____
_____
_____

What did you do for yourself today?

_____
_____
_____
_____
_____
_____
_____

What did you do for others today?

_____
_____
_____
_____
_____
_____
_____

REMEMBER ❀ REFLECT ❀ RECREATE ❀ RELATE
SHARE YOUR THOUGHTS TODAY

How did you remember, reflect, recreate, and relate today?

_____
_____
_____
_____
_____
_____
_____
_____

What did you do for yourself today?

_____
_____
_____
_____
_____
_____

What did you do for others today?

_____
_____
_____
_____
_____
_____

EMBRACE THIS NEW NORMAL

DO WHAT IS BEST FOR YOU!
WHATEVER GETS YOU THROUGH
THE MINUTE, THE HOUR, THE DAY, OR
THE MOMENT

DO WHAT IS BEST FOR YOU!

LIVE LIFE TO ITS FULLEST
YOU ARE AMAZING
YOU GOT THIS!

FIND PEACE AND PURPOSE IN
YOUR NEW NORMAL

DR. MARY WELSH | DRMARYWELSH.COM 2020